JUNGLE ANIMALS

FUN THINGS TO LOOK FOR IN THIS BOOK

LIFT-A-FACTS

Every page has two flaps that can be lifted to reveal fun facts about the animals. One flap has a fascinating fact about a physical characteristic of the animal, and the other flap tests your knowledge about the animal with a Do You Know? question.

SIZE COMPARISONS

Look for the size icon on each page. The featured animal is compared to a 4-foot tall child.

GLOSSARY WORDS

You can learn more about the meaning of certain words by looking in the glossary located in the back of the book.

Giant Day Gecko

What is a gecko? Geckos are lizards found in warm and tropical places around the world. Geckos are great climbers! The soft pads on the bottom of their feet are covered with tiny, hair–like bristles that help them hang upside down and cling to glass.

They are the **ONLY LIZARDS** that can use their **voices** to **"TALK"** with one another.

The eyelids of most geckos are see-through, like contact lenses. Geckos lick the lids to keep them clean.

Inches 0 1 2 3 4

Centimeters 0 1 2 3 4 5 6 7 8 9 10 11 12

DO YOU KNOW... what is the only known **surface** that a gecko's feet **won't** stick to?

Giant day geckos can be up to 10 inches long.

6 7 8 9 **10** 11 12 13 14 15

14 15 16 17 18 19 20 21 22 23 24 25 26 27 28 29 30 31 32 33 34 35 36 37 38

Orangutans are **not** picky eaters! Scientists have documented over **400** **types** of **foods** they eat!

Orangutan

Orangutans are members of the primate family. If you look closely, you may notice orangutans look similar to people—that's because we're primates, too! Orangutans are very smart. They spend most of their time alone in the trees of tropical rain forests. They mainly eat leaves and fruits from the trees.

Baby orangutans live with their mothers for **seven** to **eight** years. This is longer than any primate, other than humans.

DO YOU KNOW...

how many **teeth** an orangutan has?

Asian Elephant

Asian elephants live in the tropical forests of Asia. They are herbivores and eat grass, leaves, fruit, and bark from trees. They live in groups of seven to eight females, with the oldest female leading the group.

Asian elephants weigh nearly
11,000 pounds

—that's about the same weight as **four cars!**

Asian elephants **never stray far** from a source of **FRESH WATER** because they need to drink at least **ONCE A DAY.**

Elephants use their **trunks** like **straws!** They suck up **water** and then release it in their **mouths.**

DO YOU KNOW...

What **male** Asian elephants have that **females** don't?

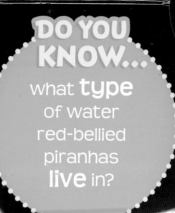

DO YOU KNOW...

what **type** of water red-bellied piranhas **live** in?

Sometimes piranhas will **join together** in **big** groups for a **FEEDING FRENZY,** **attacking** a large fish or other prey and quickly gobbling it down to the bone!

Inches
0 1 2 3 4 5 6 7 **8** 9

Centimeters
0 1 2 3 4 5 6 7 8 9 10 11 12 13 14 15 16 17 18 19 20 21 22 2

It is **very rare** for piranhas to **ATTACK** people so they **aren't** very dangerous to us.

Red-bellied Piranha

If you look at the color of this piranha's belly, you can see how it got its name. But not all red-bellied piranhas have red bellies—the coloring can be different from fish to fish, just like hair color can be different from person to person.

A **group** of **fish** is called a **school.** Red-bellied piranhas *swim* in schools.

The red-bellied piranha can grow as long as 8 to 15 inches.

10   11   12   13   14   **15**

25   26   27   28   29   30   31   32   33   34   35   36   37   38

Poison Dart Frog

This tiny frog may be one of the most beautifully colored creatures on Earth, but don't let its size and beauty fool you. These frogs have poison that is found on their skin so they are very dangerous to touch! But don't worry, you probably won't find a poisonous dart frog in your backyard, unless you live in the tropical rain forests of Costa Rica or Brazil.

Some poison dart frogs are as **tiny** as a **fingernail.**

The **bright colors** of poison dart frogs are used as a **WARNING** to predators to **STAY AWAY!**

Poison dart frogs are about one-inch long.

Inches

0	1	2	3	4

Centimeters

0	1	2	3	4	5	6	7	8	9	10	11	12

DO YOU KNOW...

what the **most poisonous** animal on Earth is?

Both the mother and father frogs **take care** of their **eggs** and **tadpoles.** Sometimes they even **carry them** on **their backs.**

Leopards are great **tree-climbers!** They can even **climb down** trees **headfirst!**

DO YOU KNOW...

what a leopard's **spots** are called?

Leopard

Leopards are big wild cats that are closely related to tigers, jaguars, and lions. Most leopards have light-colored coats with dark spots.

Leopards are great climbers and are very comfortable spending time in trees. They will often drag their prey up a tree and into the branches where they can enjoy their meal without being bothered by other hungry animals.

Leopards **communicate** in different ways. They **roar**, **growl**, and **purr**.

Mother leopards **usually give birth to two cubs at a time.**

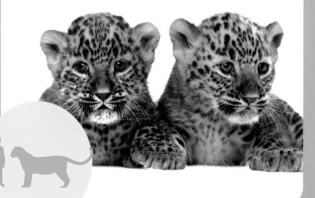

Toucan

My, what a colorful bill you have! Toucans are known for their colorful bills—the large size sometimes keeps their enemies away. But here's a secret toucans don't want their enemies to find out: their bills are not dangerous at all!

Toucans have **two** to **four babies** each year. The baby's bill is **small** at birth and grows **bigger** over several months.

Toucans **nest** in the **hollows** of trees.

DO YOU
KNOW...

what a
group
of toucans
is called?

Green tree pythons **eat birds, lizards,** and other **small reptiles.**

Pythons lay **eggs,** and may **WRAP THEMSELVES** around the eggs to **protect** them until they **hatch.**

DO YOU KNOW... why green tree pythons can eat animals **bigger** than themselves?

Green Tree Python

Look, it's a green tree python! This large, strong snake likes to hang from tree branches or curl up in them. But if you happen to be looking for one in a rain forest, you may have trouble—its green skin camouflages it from predators.

When the eggs of a green tree python **hatch,** the babies are **bright yellow, brick red** or **orange.**

Queen Alexandra's Birdwing Butterfly

Queen Alexandra's birdwing butterflies are not only pretty —they're big! They are the biggest butterflies in the world. The male butterflies have a bright yellow body and green and blue coloring in their wings. The females have brown and white wings and a cream colored body with red fur on the throat.

The Queen Alexandra's birdwing butterfly is **three times bigger** than a **monarch butterfly.**

Birdwing butterflies like to find **SUNNY** places to rest.

DO YOU KNOW...

who is **bigger,** the **male** or the **female** birdwing butterfly?

Inches 0 1 2 3 4

Centimeters 0 1 2 3 4 5 6 7 8 9 10 11 12

Female birdwing butterflies lay their **eggs** on **POISONOUS** plant leaves. When a **caterpillar hatches** from an egg, it will eat the poisonous leaf which will **keep it safe** from **predators.**

The wingspan of the birdwing butterfly extends up to 12 inches.

6　7　8　9　10　11　**12**　13　14　15

14　15　16　17　18　19　20　21　22　23　24　25　26　27　28　29　30　31　32　33　34　35　36　37　38

Glossary

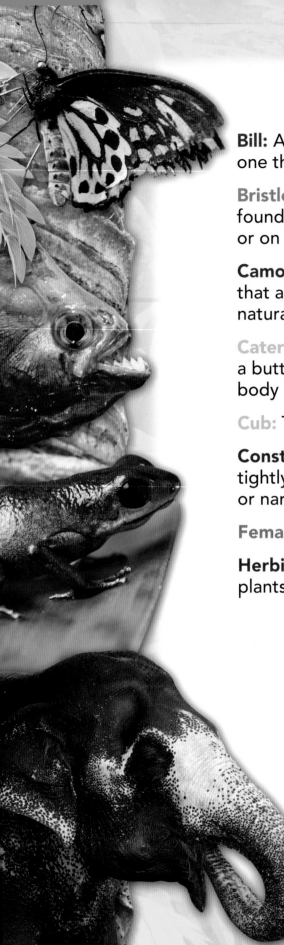

Bill: A beak of a bird, especially one that is long and slender.

Bristles: Short, stiff hair usually found on an animal's skin, a plant, or on a man's face.

Camouflage: An animal's coloring that allows it to blend in with its natural surroundings.

Caterpillar: the larva stage of a butterfly with a segmented body and three pairs of legs.

Cub: The name of a baby leopard.

Constrict: Squeezing something tightly to make it smaller or narrower.

Females: Girls

Herbivore: An animal that eats only plants.

Males: Boys

Opposable: When a thumb can touch one or more fingers on the same hand.

Poison: A dangerous substance that can cause great harm when absorbed (through drinking, eating, or injection) in a person or animal.

Predator: An animal that kills another animal for food.

Prey: An animal that is killed by another animal for food.

Primate: An animal that has hands, hand-like feet, and eyes that face forward. Humans, apes, and monkeys are all primates.

Tadpoles: The larva stage of development before becoming a frog.

Scientific Consultant

Jennifer Gresham
Director of Education
Zoo New England